THE TAO TE CHING
A paraphrase for the modern reader

Sid Millson

Copyright © 2020 by Sid Millsom

All rights reserved. This book or any portion thereof may not be reproduced or used in any manner whatsoever without the express written permission of the publisher except for the use of brief quotations in a book review.

ISBN: 978-1-944066-38-3

Printed in the United States of America

Dedication and Acknowledgments

To Kathy, for all she has done with me and for me for twenty nine years.

I also wish to acknowledge my brother, Charles, and my good friends, Brian and Robert.

Preface

I do not speak, read, or write any dialect of Chinese, so this cannot correctly be called a translation of the Tao Te Ching. Instead, it is a paraphrase, a loose rendering of my own interpretation of the meaning of the Tao. This book represents the *ideals* of the Tao stated in twenty-first century *ideas*.

I had three goals in mind as I wrote:

1. I wanted to share the wisdom of the Tao Te Ching in a way that was accessible to as many people as possible.

2. I wanted to make the Tao Te Ching as gender neutral as possible.

3. I wanted to remove from the Tao as many references to war and political conflict as I could, and make it more applicable to the

everyday reader. There are places that the Tao Te Ching gives advice to government officials and rulers regarding how to wage war. I personally, did not find this appropriate for the reader I was trying to reach. I changed these references to leadership in general, and hopefully preserved the original intent of the text.

I have enjoyed reading the Tao Te Ching for years, however I would not say that I agree with or endorse the entire document. I have tried to not allow that to color my interpretation of it, paraphrasing the sections that I did not agree with as faithfully as possible.

In writing this paraphrase, I have relied on **The Tao and Its Characteristics, a Translation of the Tao Te Ching,** by James Legge (1891), as my primary source.

Introduction

The Tao Te Ching is a short book that deals with a big subject - the nature of the universe and how to live in it. It was written by a person named Lao Tzu (or Laozi) in southern China sometime in the sixth century BCE.

Little is known about Lao Tzu. Some doubt he existed at all and attribute the Tao to many writers over a period of years. Most, however, believe that he was a teacher-philosopher of China's royal court or an employee of the court. He grew tired of the greed and arrogance he saw and how little good was accomplished because of those attitudes. Frustrated, he left the royal city with the intent of heading west into the high mountains of Himalaya. Before reaching the wilderness he was asked by his followers to record his teachings for others to study. For two days he sat and wrote the eighty-one verses of the Tao Te Ching, much of it as poetry.

Lao Tzu's philosophy remained just that, a philosophy, and did not become a religion for centuries. The time during which it was followed as a religious belief is referred to as the "dark ages" of Taoism.

The Taoist philosophy has four loosely defined concepts:

1. The **First Principle** states that everything in nature is all part of the same whole.

2. **Wu Wei** is the principle of non-action. The idea is that doing nothing accomplishes everything.

3. Opposites are needed in order for harmony to exist in the universe. These opposites are often referred to as **Yin** and **Yang**.

4. Perhaps most characteristic of Taoism is the concept of **Pu**. Pu is beautifully illustrated by the statement that a living tree is more beautiful and useful than anything that can be carved from its wood.

The term "Tao" is often translated as "the way" or "the path," but it can also mean "the teaching." Several chapters of the Tao Te Ching speak of the Tao as the "mystery of mysteries" and this phrase, maybe more than any other, carries the weight of this ancient philosophy.

The Tao Te Ching divides its writings between two simple yet profound ideas. First, Lao Tzu writes about the idea that life and the entire universe is a mystery that can never be completely explained or understood. Because of this unattainable mystery, Lao Tzu compares life to a river and encourages all of humanity to float the river rather than fight the current. Second, the Tao Te Ching encourages us to just let go, to do nothing to promote ourselves. It teaches us to give up ego and let go of our appetites and live just in the moment.

By pursuing both of these goals we become better human beings and better able to serve others.

I commend this philosophy to you and hope, as did Lao Tzu that you are encouraged by reading.

ONE

If you are walking a path that is easy, you are probably not on the right path. If you know where your path is going, that is also probably not the right path.

The path you should be walking is both known and shrouded in great mystery. This mystery path is the very core of the universe, and the part that is known is all that you see around you.

If you get to the point where you desire none of those things you see, then you will understand the nature of the mystery. And that mystery is the key to all you need to know.

TWO

You only know what is beautiful because you have seen things that are not so beautiful. You only know what is good because you have seen things that are evil. Many things are like this. Extremes are often used as comparison: difficult and easy, long and short, high and low, before and after. Some people are baffled by this, but the wise people use it to their advantage.

Wise people take care of things they do not own. They work when there is no paycheck, and they compete without rewards.

The person who never demands honor will never be dishonored.

THREE

If you are always trying to keep up appearances, do not be surprised if you remain discontented. It is only the valuable things that you have to hide. If you never display anything of value then you never have to worry about having anything stolen.

There is a paradox that only the wise person knows: the way to control people is by not trying to control anyone at all. Rather than trying to control them, look out for their best interest instead.

Sometimes doing nothing is the best thing you can do. And when you do something make sure you do it with a selfless and pure motive. This is the path that leads to contentment.

FOUR

The mystery is both full and empty, the child of everyone and the ancestor of all.

    It is like a cloud with soft edges whose rain settles the dust.

    It is hiding in plain sight.
It is without mother and father, but related to everyone.

FIVE

The universe could care very little about the things you accumulate. Wise people therefore are not attached to things and only to very few people.

Wise people think like the universe. They nether regard nor disregard those around them. Any gift that they give has no strings attached, offering what they have to anyone who has need.

In the middle of the universe is a place that is both empty and full. It both gives and is given to.

Find common ground. You can do nothing better than to be still and listen to your own truth.

SIX

Your emotions are always with you in the same way that your mother is with you for life. When you are young, your mother's teachings are your gateway to your adult life.

Do not be afraid of emotions. Listen to them in the same way as you would listen to your mother. She has much to teach you and her advice will never fail you.

SEVEN

The sky provides the rain so that the earth can provide our food. They do not do this for us; they do it because they always have from the beginning.

The wise people go about their tasks with the same sort of detachment. Because they are detached they are also one with all. That is how you find fulfillment in your every day actions.

EIGHT

Life should be like water. Water sustains life. It can flow through anything and yet it appears weak and in that way it is like the great mystery.

When choosing where to live, make it simple.

When you meditate, think deeply.

When you interact with others, be gentle and kind.

When you speak, tell the truth.

When you make decisions, seek justice.

Always do the right thing at the right time.

If you avoid conflict, you will avoid blame.

NINE

If you continue to pour after the cup is full, you are wasting the tea. If you continue to sharpen the blade after the blade is already sharp, the edge will soon disappear.

If you continue to gain wealth after you already have enough, you will never feel secure. Disaster will follow after pride.

When you have done all you can do, stop. Overdoing anything will often ruin it. This is all part of the mystery.

TEN

Do you understand that your body and the life that inhabits it cannot be separated? Can you relax your body and be like an infant in your comings and goings, and just love yourself?

Likewise as a leader, can you love those you lead without needing praise? Treat others as a mother treats her children, without taking credit, leading without the need to be out front.

If you understand this then you are beginning to make the mystery plain and simple.

ELEVEN

A wheel is made up of the tire, spokes, and the hub, but it is the empty space in the center that connects to the axle that gives the wheel its usefulness. So it is with a cup. It is the empty space inside the cup that makes the cup useful. Doors and windows are the same way; it is the space they open up that make them valuable. This is how it is with life. What is not there may be more important than what is there.

TWELVE

Overindulgence can muffle your senses, as can rushing around trying to gain wealth.

Wise people do not discount their intuition when making life choices.

THIRTEEN

Bad things will happen. Learn to accept those experiences as part of every person's life.

Embrace the idea that you matter very little in the big scheme of things. So do not try to keep score of your successes or failures.

You have a physical body and bodies feel pain sometimes. No body, no pain, but also, no body, no life. So accept pain as an indicator that you are alive.

Recognize your place in the natural world and see yourself as a servant of nature. After all, the world supports you, so you can support it.

FOURTEEN

The mystery is something that defies the senses. It cannot be seen. It cannot be heard. It cannot be held.

If you look at it from the earth, it looks like the sky. If you look down at it from the sky, it looks like the earth. It is beyond description. It comes from nothing and returns to nothing. It cannot be defined and it defies imagination.

You cannot trace it to its beginnings and you cannot follow it to its end. But, do not give up on the mystery, you will find it in the present.

Today is the beginning of the mystery.

FIFTEEN

Those in the past who have grasped the mystery were wise beyond comprehension. There is no need to describe them because you know them by their deeds.

They were cautious like someone walking across a frozen river, alert and aware. Yet, they were simple as a block of wood. They emptied themselves and became like water, taking the shape of the world around them. Out of that water life arose.

Those who have found the mystery are first like sprouting seeds, then growing plants and finally they bring forth fruit. This all happens in due time.

SIXTEEN

Guard your quiet times and quiet spaces with all your might. In your comings and goings, return to those times and spaces as often as you can if you want to flourish like a luxurious tropical plant.

It is our desire to find peace and consistency in our lives and return to that place as often as we can. This is the heart of wisdom. Finding peace and consistency will help you avoid trouble in the long run.

Finding this consistency will lead you to fairness. Fairness will lead you into a sense of community with the world. This oneness with the world will give you a timelessness and that is the very heart of the mystery.

SEVENTEEN

There are four types of leaders:

    Leaders who are despised,

    Leaders who are feared,

    Leaders who are barely known,

    And leaders who are loved.

    Leaders who do not trust are not trusted.

A good leader accomplishes things so that the followers say, "look what we have done."

EIGHTEEN

When the mystery is forgotten, people are motivated by a sense of obligation. When they lose their sense of obligation towards one another, it is replaced by insincerity and hypocrisy.

When you cannot solve you own problems, there is always someone who is willing to step in and solve them for you. Individuals often surrender their free will to families. Families often surrender their free will to the government.

NINETEEN

If we could give up subtlety in exchange for common sense we would all be better off.

If we could give up rules about living and just treat each other with kindness we would all be better off.

While you are at it, give up "get rich quick" schemes and you will do away with a lot of crime.

All these kinds of things are outward replacements for inner principles. They only create burdens in your life. Seek simplicity. Live a simple life and you will avoid trouble.

TWENTY

Make sure that you know the difference between intelligence and knowledge.

Also know the difference between a "yes" that is sincere and a "yes" just said to get a pat on the back. They are the same words, but mean very different things.

Everyone faces fears in life, but do not let your fear control you.

Most people are content with enough to eat and drink. I, however, am not sure what it will take to satisfy me. So, I will keep searching, even at the cost of looking like a failure, a homeless wanderer. I will search even if it means that I look foolish and confused.

Ordinary people's lives look ordered and wise. Those on a quest for the great mystery will appear lost as if adrift on the sea.

Everyone has a purpose; mine is the unending quest for the great original mystery.

TWENTY-ONE

The great mystery is the source of strength for all you do.

This mystery cannot be seen or touched and yet it forms our whole reality, all we see and touch.

This is the paradox: the mystery is profound but it is also profoundly simple. It lights your path with simple truth. It contains all truth, all knowledge since the beginning of time, and is empty at the same time.

How, then, do you come to understand it? By letting the mystery itself be your mentor.

TWENTY-TWO

The mystery is all about paradox.

Empty yourself to be full.

Surrender to win.

Give away to gain.

Desire nothing and gain more.

Wise people understand this and only embrace the mystery itself. Even though they do not live for praise they receive it for their simple life. Without bragging, the wise receive recognition for their wisdom. Others look to wise people for direction.

This synergy is an ancient idea… the whole is greater than the sum of its parts.

TWENTY-THREE

When you speak, keep it short. A strong storm does not last long. If the weather can figure this out so should you.

When you find others who are trying to understand the mystery, make every effort to find places where you have common ground. Even if you disagree with their interpretation of the mystery, still find some point of agreement.

Living in harmony with the mystery and others who are searching for it will bring you happiness.

If you trust the process then the process will work for everyone.

TWENTY-FOUR

Be content. Do not try to be more or less than yourself. You cannot be taller, shorter, smarter or anything else by just pretending to be so for the praise of others. Living that way only makes you appear broken or silly to those around you.

Those who are truly living in the mystery have a deep satisfaction with who they are.

TWENTY-FIVE

From the beginning of the universe this mystery has existed. It just may be that the universe itself came to be because of this mystery. As the universe has expanded and changed, this mystery remains unchanged.

We do not know the name of the mystery, but if we had to call it something we might call it "the path" or "the way." Whatever you call it, it is the great mystery.

It is like a comet. It appears bright for a while and then becomes dim but it will always come back.

There are four great powers on earth: wisdom, the sky, the earth and this great mystery.

You might say that human beings are at the mercy of the earth. The earth is at the mercy of the sky. The sky is at the mercy of the great mystery.

TWENTY-SIX

Heavy and light, stillness and motion, each is appropriate in its own time.

Travelers are cautious with their luggage until they arrive at their destination and can lock their valuables away. After this the vacation can begin.

Anyone with responsibilities needs to take them seriously. Decisions made in a hurry or without serious thought can cost you.

TWENTY-SEVEN

This is what simple wisdom looks like:

The wise traveler leaves no footsteps.

The wise speaker says nothing that needs further explanation.

The wise businessperson needs no accountant.

It is like a door built so strongly that it needs no locks, or a rope so strong that needs no knots.

The wise person leaves no one behind. Everyone is important. This is vital to understanding the mystery.

Every time people meet there are teachers and learners. When you recognize this, and your role as either teacher or learner, you are honoring the great mystery.

TWENTY-EIGHT

If you want to get to the root of the earth then embrace the characteristics of both genders. If you do this you will have the best of both worlds and you become like a child again when gender did not matter.

Finding the balance between darkness and light will show the world your character. It will also give you unlimited options, as opposed to the limited options of one extreme or the other.

The root of the world can be found by embracing your mistakes. This will also show the world your true character.

Which is more beautiful, a carving made of wood or the tree from which the wood came? A wise leader will remember to honor both the tree and the carving, the humble and the exalted.

TWENTY-NINE

Be very careful before you consider changing the world. The world is a precious thing and any change to it needs to come with great consideration. That which we try to change we often damage and that which we try to grasp often slips through our fingers.

The world is full of extremes: hot and cold, strong and weak, leaders and followers. Wise people avoid extremes and seek the middle ground. Extremes are the easy path; the middle ground is the difficult way.

THIRTY

When you give advice to anyone, especially a leader, make sure that the advice you give is in harmony with the great mystery. All your advice to anyone should lean toward gentleness. It is through gentleness that we get the most done.

Anger grows like weeds and arguments can leave relationships hurting like parched ground. Good leaders reach gentle solutions without using force.

Good leaders make hard decisions without being condescending. These decisions are made once, out of necessity, and not out of pride.

Living in harmony with the great mystery may lead you to a long life.

THIRTY-ONE

Those who are trying to understand the great mystery would do well to avoid anger and certainly violence.

Wise people recognize that there are two sides to every problem and many possible solutions. Anger and violence are never the first choice. Approach life calmly and with a hope to create peace. Any other way may leave lasting damage to relationships that you value. Never find joy in controversy.

Good leaders surround themselves with good advisers. Some advise during times of trouble, and some advise during times of plenty. Leaders who have had to make hard decisions understand the gravity of those decisions and how they affect the lives of the followers.

THIRTY-TWO

The great mystery never changes. It is profound and yet profoundly simple. Those who understand it will have the earth and sky at their fingertips. It will be as if weather itself obeys their command.

While the mystery can never be fully understood, those who seek to understand it begin to see the advantage in the search. The mystery is like a great river flowing to the sea. The source of the river may be a mystery but we can still drink the water.

THIRTY-THREE

Before you try to know anyone else, first make sure you understand yourself. Before you try to fight another's battle, find peace with yourself.

If you can push away from the table and say "enough," then you will never be hungry. Be content with what you have and be content with where you are. If you want to have immortality then leave your mark while you are alive.

THIRTY-FOUR

Look around you and you will see that the great mystery is everywhere. It permeates all things and gives life to all things. The great mystery is always hovering just in the background, never seeking prominence. It is like a leader who does not wear a suit but wears jeans instead. The great mystery moves in cycles, appearing and disappearing. It exists and yet it has no name.

Wise people follow the example of the great mystery, quietly doing their job and quietly making a difference. They accomplish great things without a great stir.

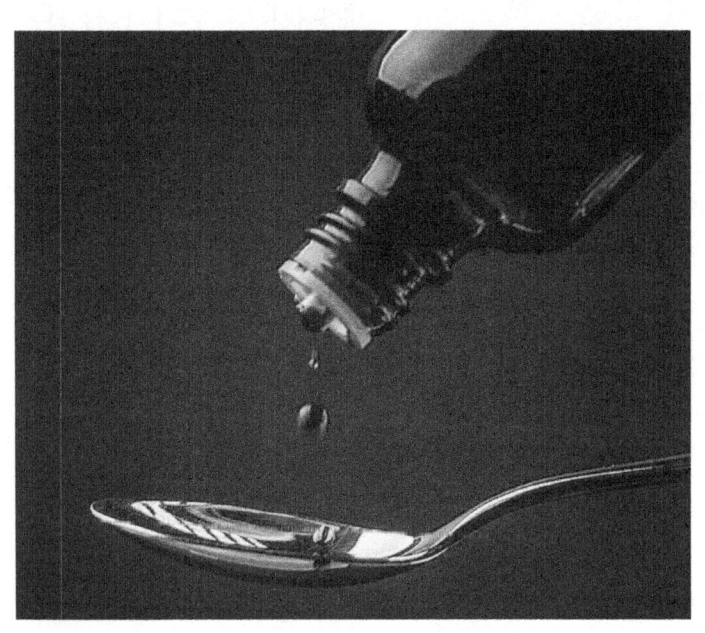

THIRTY-FIVE

Those who hold the great mystery in their hands will find that the world will come to them for guidance and peace. They will understand that you offer them only good and not harm.

The temptation to give up the search for meaning in the mystery is like hearing the sounds and smelling the smells of a party - you want to stop and enjoy. While the great mystery may not "taste good," its benefits are immeasurable.

THIRTY-SIX

All of life is like the tides:

    Coming in and going out.

    Breathing in and breathing out.

    Winning and losing.

    Hiding and finding.

    Giving gifts and receiving gifts.

Often you find that the weak overcomes the strong, and the soft overcomes the hard. Everything has its appropriate place; fish belong in the water and birds belong in the air.

THIRTY-SEVEN

The great mystery teaches us that the greatest deeds are accomplished with the least effort. Leaders would do well to learn this lesson. It will completely change how they lead. Leading with this type of simplicity will not only accomplish more, it will also increase the loyalty of your followers.

With no desire for praise, people go about their business with a new intensity.

THIRTY-EIGHT

Those who have no understanding of the great mystery seem to have a need to be seen and noticed. Those who are beginning to understand the mystery need less attention in their lives. Those who have the greatest understanding of the mystery do not need to be noticed at all; their ego is all but nonexistent. They go to great links to accomplish their tasks without fanfare or praise.

The mystery teaches us to be ethical and help others without expectations.

When we fail to acknowledge the great mystery, good deeds and ethical behavior are still accomplished, but they are accomplished with a desire for attention and notoriety.

As we move away from the great mystery, real humility and real empathy become harder and harder to recognize. These qualities are replaced by pageantry which is the beginning of chaos. It is like a plant that has beautiful flowers and yet bears no edible fruit. Wise people avoid this and seek the steadfastness of the great mystery.

THIRTY-NINE

The sky is clear because of the great mystery. The earth is secure because of the great mystery. Our consciousness depends on the great mystery. Even farmlands bring forth their crops because of the mystery. Nature depends on it. Leaders lead because of it. Life itself depends on the great mystery.

Without the great mystery the sky is dim. Without the great mystery the earth trembles. Without the great mystery we are brute beasts. Without the great mystery croplands fail. Without the great mystery leaders struggle and there is confusion. Without the great mystery life suffers.

So find affirmation in humility and find strength in your weakness. Leaders, find your voice in silence. Do not consider those you lead to be your servants doing your bidding. Rather consider them as co-leaders, working with you to accomplish goals. Just as a ship is made of a rudder, a sail and a hull, so each member of the group plays an important role.

FORTY

The great mystery moves in cycles, going forward and retreating as the need arises.

The great mystery gives birth to everything, and in death everything returns to it.

FORTY-ONE

The "A student" is immersed in understanding the mystery. The "C student" spends a little time focused on the mystery. The student that struggles ignores the mystery altogether, or worse, finds the mystery a source of derision.

Compared to the great mystery...

The brightest light seems dim.

The straightest road seems crooked.

The highest mountain seems like a valley.

What is considered beautiful seems repulsive.

A square seems round.

The loudest sound seems like a whisper.

Compared to the great mystery all images seem blurry.

The great mystery is just that, a mystery, but it gives meaning to all of life.

FORTY-TWO

The great mystery progresses as steadily as one, two three. This progression encompasses great extremes: light and dark, quiet and loud, introvert and extrovert.

No one wants to be alone in the world. No one wants to feel as if they have no value. But there are those who long for the "anonymity of humility." There is a saying, "sometimes you win and sometimes you lose." We wish life was not this way, but it seems to be true.

Angry young people usually become angry old people. There is nothing new about that statement. The key to this whole teaching is that doing the same things in the same ways will always give you the same results.

FORTY-THREE

The soft and pliable will ultimately overcome that which is rigid and hard. Just as water can penetrate every crevice in a stone wall, there is an advantage to doing nothing and "letting nature take its course."

Wise people learn without being taught and there is an advantage to that.

FORTY-FOUR

Who would trade their life for being famous or who would trade their life for being rich? Keep your life and lose everything else. Those other things only bring sorrow and pain.

Those who seek fame and wealth have no time to find what is really important. When you are content you have no fear, no shame, no blame and no danger. Contentment leads to a long and happy life.

FORTY-FIVE

When you understate your achievements those who see your efforts will be pleasantly surprised.

That which seems full is empty.

That which seems straight is crooked.

That which seems wise is foolish.

If it is cold, keep moving. If it is hot, hold still.

The only law the world needs is the law of quiet simplicity.

FORTY-SIX

When, finally, the great mystery is understood by all, machines used for war will become farming equipment. Tanks will be plowing the fields.

Blind ambition and discontent will lead to greed and disregard of the needs of others. Both of these are what have started most wars in the first place - getting instead of giving. Be content with what you have.

FORTY-SEVEN

When you understand your own mind, you begin to understand the world outside you. Without walking out your door or looking out your window, you know the world, because you know yourself. The more removed you are from yourself the less you understand others.

Wise people can gain wisdom without traveling. They can understand other cultures without visiting them. Wise people find meaning in life with little effort.

FORTY-EIGHT

A person who seeks information gains something every day. A person who tries to understand the great mystery loses something every day. This is all done on purpose, simplifying life every day until the point is reached where nothing is done but nothing is left undone.

If you feel that the world owes you something, this will only lead to trouble for you and for the world. If you want "what is coming to you," be very careful because it is on the way.

FORTY-NINE

Empathy comes from a center of personal strength.

It is easy to show kindness to those who are kind to you. It is more difficult to show kindness to those who are mean to you. Be genuine with others even when they are not genuine with you.

To the foolish, wise people can appear disoriented and indecisive. Those who are seeking wisdom are drawn to wise people like curious children.

FIFTY

Everybody is born and everybody dies. If you take ten human beings you will find that three of the ten are content. Another three of the ten are just trudging along until death. Another three are rushing through life from birth to death because they want to get as much out of life as they can.

Only one of these ten people really knows how to live, wandering through life without fear. This one does not fear natural disasters or fear man-made disasters. How can this be? This one knows death is real, but has somehow learned not to fear death.

FIFTY-ONE

The great mystery is responsible for and sustains all of creation. When you realize that your existence depends on the mystery then you will begin to pursue it and to desire to understand it. Wise people respect and rely on this flow of life-giving energy.

This respect is not a religion but a willing testimony of the power of the great mystery.

The mystery not only creates, but also feeds, clothes, heals, cares for and nurtures all of life as would a parent. This "mysterious shelter" does its job without thanks or recognition.

FIFTY-TWO

The mystery is the parent of all you observe. As good children, we care for the aging parent and protect that parent from all harm for the rest of our lives.

The lives of humble people are free from care, but there is no safe place for those who brag about their accomplishments.

Pay attention to details and you will know the secret of a clear mind. Support those who are gentle and you will find strength.

FIFTY-THREE

If I were to suddenly become a popular leader, the thing that would scare me most is that I would begin to take myself seriously. The way to avoid this pitfall is to keep your focus on the great mystery.

The great mystery is a simple path but it is not an easy one. For this reason many people avoid it and choose another way.

Sometimes the lives of people are like a beautiful mansion with the lawn not mowed. They wear the finest clothes, eat the best food and own the most expensive things. While there is nothing wrong with these things, it often causes you to lose your focus on the great mystery.

FIFTY-FOUR

A garden that is properly tended will nurture its plants for years. It will feed your children and your grandchildren.

If you plant good values in your heart you will gain integrity. If you plant these values in your family, they will be a blessing to you. If you plant good values in your community, you give it a good foundation. If you plant good values in your country then the citizens will always have what they need. If you plant these same values in the whole world, there will be peace.

See others as you see yourself. See other communities as you see your own community. See other countries as you view your own country View the world as part of the whole universe.

How do you know this will work? Try it and see.

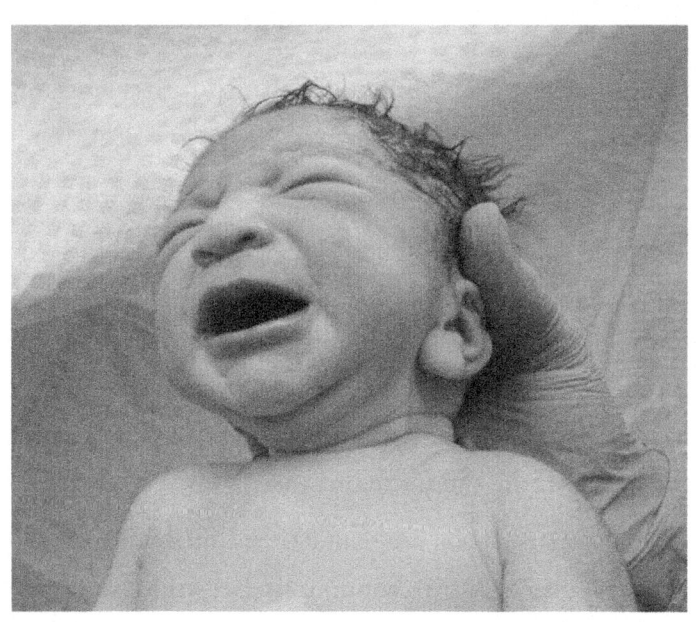

FIFTY-FIVE

When you begin to understand the great mystery, you become like a newborn baby. Just like a baby is protected from harm by its parents so the great mystery will protect you. Like babies we will be weak and helpless, but also like babies we will learn something new every day. And although a newborn baby knows very little about relationships, it still knows that it wants to be loved. Even the cries of a baby are for the harmony relationship.

The great mystery produces a sort of music in the universe. This music leads to a consistency. Consistency leads to wisdom, and it is wisdom that sits on the throne. Anything we do to overturn this progression leads to disharmony in the song of the universe. Let the mystery play its own tune.

No matter how strong we are, all of us will grow old. This is part of the wisdom of the great mystery. Everything else will come to an end.

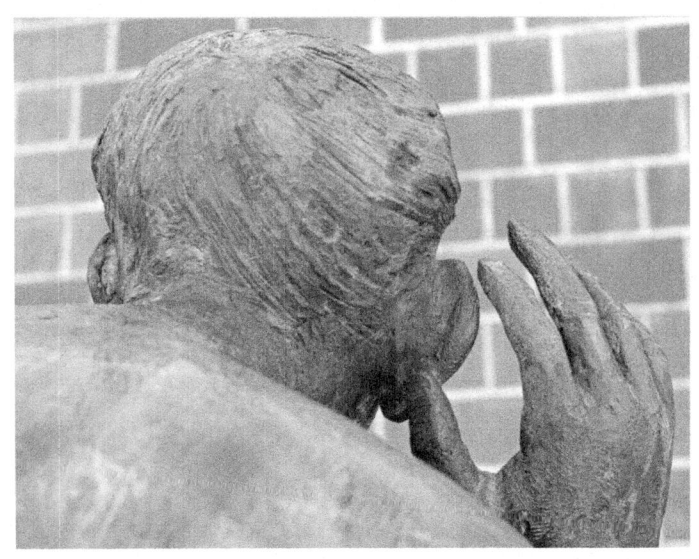

FIFTY-SIX

Those who understand the great mystery understand that it cannot be explained. Those who try to explain the great mystery do not truly understand it.

When you understand the great mystery you will simplify your life. You will speak less and listen more. The great mystery will soften life's rough edges. It will dim life's glaring lights. Everywhere you look you will find evidence of the great mystery.

It is difficult to put a label on those who understand this mystery. They are neither aloof nor familiar. They are neither rich nor poor. They are neither a follower not a leader. However, there is something that is remarkable about them.

FIFTY-SEVEN

Show mercy in your decisions. End arguments quickly.

If you truly want to sit on top of the world, do nothing.

Be simple in your leadership. The more rules and regulations a leader has, the less the followers are benefited by the leadership. Even when you think those rules and regulations are benefiting the followers, they will still get in the way of what you are trying to accomplish. Cliques and gossip will dominate the group. You may think rules and regulations lead to more organization; it really leads to more confusion.

A true leader is organic in leadership style so that the group manages themselves. This kind of leadership will lead to a sense of peace and fairness. The efforts of the followers will not be interfered with and purposes will be accomplished. A true leader leads without ambition and with a sense of simplicity.

FIFTY-EIGHT

If you want people around you to be relaxed then you be relaxed. If you want people to feel like they have to sneak around you, then keep a strong grip on them.

Happiness and sadness are two sides of the same coin. You never know what lies around the corner so do not take either one too seriously.

Do not stress too much during the hard times, because good times will soon follow. And, do not get too excited during the good times because it will not be long before the days get long and hard again.

Wise people are not harsh. They injure no one either with words or with actions. Wise people are honest without being brutal. They shine a light into the world without blinding it.

FIFTY-NINE

As a leader, if you want to achieve great things while at the same time avoiding grave mistakes then find the middle ground. It is at this middle place where we do our best work. It is also the place where the great mystery can be found. It is from the center that the most can be accomplished. In fact there is limitless opportunity when you find your own center.

If you want your leadership to endure and grow roots then lead like a parent would lead a child. This will give your leadership a lasting vision. This is the great mystery.

SIXTY

Leading a large group is like cooking a small fish; it is a delicate process.

If you approach life from the perspective of the great mystery, life will be different. It is not that evil will cease to exist, but that evil will lose its footing. You will not harm anyone and no one will harm you. This kind of harmony with life comes from living in harmony with the great mystery.

SIXTY-ONE

If an organization wants to be great then it needs to be like a great river. It flows to the ocean, enriching all along its banks.

The soft and gentle can overcome the hard and rough by being subtle.

The large can gain the trust of the small and the small can gain the favor of the large. This kind of relationship can be attained by both parties practicing humility. The large is only trying to expand and the small is trying to protect itself. Each gets what it desires by setting ego aside.

SIXTY-TWO

The great mystery sits in the center of the universe. Both good and bad encompass it.

If you speak wisely you will be respected, but if you act wisely you will be loved. If you are unkind you will be abandoned.

If you were offered the whole world, priceless jewels and all kinds of luxuries, none of it would compare to the understanding of the great mystery.

From the beginning of time wise people have sought out the mystery. If you seek it, you will find it, without guilt or shame. This is the true worth of the great mystery.

SIXTY-THREE

When you live according to the great mystery you will act without focusing on acting. You will accomplish without trying to accomplish. That which is small will be great. That which is few will be many. That which others consider to be unkind you will accept as kindness.

When you live according to the great mystery, that which is difficult will seem easy. That which is great will seem small. Yes, the great will seem small, and the small will seem great. This is why wise people never consider the greatness of a task but simply go about accomplishing it.

If you make a promise lightly you probably will not keep it. You will always find a reason to be doing something else. This is why wise people never make promises unless they intend on keeping them, and then nothing will prevent them from fulfilling their duty.

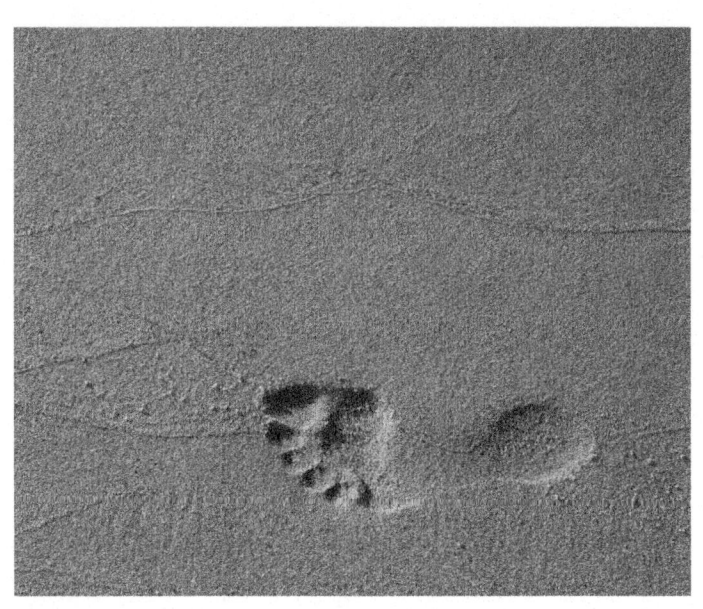

SIXTY-FOUR

Be proactive. Take matters in hand before they get out of hand. Deal with a problem before it gets too big. Small issues are easier to deal with than big ones. Solve a crisis before it is a crisis. Seek order before things get out of order.

A large oak tree grows from a tiny acorn and a great building begins with a foundation. A journey of a thousand kilometers begins with a single step.

If your motives are wrong, you will do harm, even if you think you will not. If you grab a thing too tightly, it will slip away from you. This is why wise people examine their motives before they take action. They do not take hold of anything without a sure grip. Be as careful at the end of a process as you are at the beginning, otherwise you might miss an opportunity for success.

Wise people do not seek the same sort of successes as others. They avoid complicating their lives but are content with what others look down on. In this way they live harmoniously with the universe by never acting with selfish intent.

SIXTY-FIVE

Understanding the great mystery is a task for the individual. It is not your place to explain it to anyone else. People must be humble and remove complications from their lives before they have the ability to understand life.

True leadership does not lead with the mind only, but also with the heart. Otherwise you are failing as a leader. When you lead with your heart, considering the emotional needs of the people, you will be a blessing to them. This is the true standard for leadership and understanding that standard forms a delicate balance of heart and mind.

The great mystery is deep, even preposterous, but when understood leads to a deep sense of peace.

SIXTY-SIX

The ocean is lower in elevation than all the rivers and streams on earth. Yet the oceans receive the water from every river and stream. If you want to receive what the world has to offer, you must be like the ocean and humble yourself and then the world will give up its treasures to you.

If you want to be a leader, be humble and the people will give you their devotion. Even though you are the leader, those whom you lead will not see you as a burden. Even though you are out in front, you will not block their view of the goal they are trying to reach. A good leader does not antagonize his followers but nurtures them.

The world will not grow weary of this type of leader. A leader like this will not resist and therefore will not be resisted.

SIXTY-SEVEN

Because the great mystery is neither complex nor full of dogma, it is often seen as insignificant. However, it is that very simplicity that makes the great mystery so significant.

There are three things that I consider to be of the greatest importance: gentleness, simplicity and humility. Gentleness allows me to relate well to others. Simplicity gives me opportunity to help others. Humility grants me the ability to honor others. Granted these three ideas are very different from other dogmas and philosophies.

It might seem counter intuitive, but gentleness is the best self-defense and the best way to secure yourself in the world.

SIXTY-EIGHT

Good leaders are not confrontational, nor are they easily angered. But because they are humble their leadership is rarely challenged.

Throughout history great leaders treated all people with respect. In this way conflict is avoided. This is true nobility.

SIXTY-NINE

Never start an argument just to advance your cause. Always behave around others as if you are a guest in their home. Yes, it is better to back away from an argument than to rush headlong into it. Sometimes if you appear strong or if your position is unknown you may avoid an argument.

It is very sad to attack someone without provocation. Gentleness is so precious that it is a shame to give it up just to exhibit power. The only way to win a confrontation is to avoid it.

SEVENTY

The things I have been saying are not hard to understand, even visualize, but they are very difficult to put it into practice.

There is a central theme to everything I have been saying, a core principle that is at the heart of my teaching. If you do not understand this central theme then you will not understand me as a teacher.

Those who would understand my teaching are few, but that does not diminish the value of that teaching.

Wise people dress very simply and keep their valuables well hidden.

SEVENTY-ONE

To know how much you do not know is the highest education. To not know what you do not know is a disease.

If you recognize the symptoms of this disease you are beginning to be healed from it. Wise people know the pain that this disease causes and therefore avoid it.

SEVENTY-TWO

There are things that all people should fear. When we are not afraid of those things we are in danger of them coming upon us.

Do not be satisfied with the ordinary. At the same time do not get tired of living your everyday life. Both of these are characteristics of emotional laziness.

Wise people are introspective without being self indulgent. They respect themselves without being arrogant. They maintain a healthy balance on all of these things.

SEVENTY-THREE

If you dare to break the rules, then be prepared to accept the consequences. Be bold enough to accept the rules and follow them. Then the consequences will not matter to you. The advantage will almost always go to those wise enough to keep the rules.

The great mystery overcomes adversity with no effort. It makes its point without speaking. It calls to no one, but everyone is drawn to it. The great mystery makes no plans but accomplishes its mission.

The great mystery casts a large net that catches all people.

SEVENTY-FOUR

If you can overcome your fear of death, then those who would use that fear as a weapon against you, lose all control over your life. There are those who, right or wrong, use the fear of death as a weapon.

There are those who have perfected this fear tactic and are strategic in their use of this power. Others are like amateurs and only scare themselves.

SEVENTY-FIVE

When you take from the needs of others to satisfy your own wants everyone suffers.

When you find that people are hard to lead you might well examine the qualities of the leader. Often the problem lies with the leader and not the followers when things are not accomplished. When the burdens placed upon the people are too great, they lose hope and cannot see the vision of the leader. The answer is not to minimize the vision but rather to maximize the leadership.

SEVENTY-SIX

We are small and weak at our birth. We are large and strong when we grow up, but then we age and die. Trees and plants begin life as tiny seeds. They grow to become strong, but soon dry, wither and die.

It seems that death is associated with great size and strength, while life is associated with weakness and small size.

Do not think that you will win with strength. Just as a big tree is an invitation to the trimmer, your strength will invite calamities.

The large and strong will give way to the small and weak.

SEVENTY-SEVEN

The great mystery is like bending a bow to release an arrow. The ends bend toward the middle to gain strength. So it is that strength comes when extremes move toward the center and compromise is reached.

This is also true with kindness. Those who have extreme abundance will gain strength by moving toward those of extreme poverty. Those who do not understand the great mystery will not understand this.

Great leaders motivate others to act with no need of recognition for themselves. Even when they gain recognition, they give others the credit.

SEVENTY-EIGHT

There is nothing as soft and weak as water. Yet, look what a flood can do to the landscape. There is no force in nature that compares to water.

Soft overcomes hard, and weak overcomes strong. Ideally we understand this, but practically it is difficult to achieve.

Wise leaders understand that they must bear the burden of failure. When leaders take responsibility for mistakes and failures, they receive the respect of the followers. This is a paradox of the great mystery.

SEVENTY-NINE

When two people argue and then make peace, there can still be hard feelings between the two. The way to avoid this is to allow the other person the dignity of being right.

Even if you feel that you have won the argument never force your opinion. As a matter of fact, you are generally always better off to keep your opinion to yourself.

The great mystery shows no partiality to any opinion. It only favors love.

EIGHTY

Just because you think yourself insignificant, that does not mean your options are limited. It just means that you must count the cost carefully before implementing any of them. Do not make big changes in a hurry.

Be content with what you have and give up trying to keep up with those you think have more. Be self-sufficient.

EIGHT-ONE

Sometimes the most meaningful thing you can say is not the kindest, and the kindest thing said may not have much meaning.

Those who understand the great mystery do not argue about it. They understand that it means different things to different people. Those who understand the great mystery are not arrogant about their understanding.

Wise people understand the paradox of sharing. The more you accumulate for yourself the less you have, and the more you give to others the more you will have.

The great mystery is very plain, but does not force itself on others. It comes freely to those wise enough to receive it.

Made in the USA
Monee, IL
06 January 2021